US Naturalized Citizen

US Naturalized Citizen

Korean experiences and American experiences
(Documentary)

Dorothy M. Hong

iUniverse, Inc.
Bloomington

US Naturalized Citizen
Korean experiences and American experiences

Author is not making a judgment or assessment or for that matter commenting about relatedness in transactions or correlations among Crazy Eddie shareholder suit, Bernie Madoff, Ezra Merkin, Whitewater (Hillary Clinton), Snow Boarding (GW Bush), Forsyth Park in Savannah, GA rantings, DePietro case relating to kidnappings in Cross County Mall in Yonkers or Chinese CFTC case in Oklahoma, Tsunami in Sendai for Japanese investors being able to over-ride clawback provisions and redeem from their hedge funds investments or contractors earning wrap fees tantamount to thuggery or restaurant application on facebook. Hazzebollah as a terror group is posted on Wikipedia and Patriot Group as hate group is posted on Southern Poverty Law Center (Richard Cohen).

Prof. Christine Choy of NYU Film who is cc'ed here [in my e-mail to iUniverse] may be able to shed some light on this matter.

As a case for Korean studies/history, I have drafted in an abstract manner as is normally the case in East Asian Studies situations.

iUniverse books may be ordered through booksellers or by contacting:

iUniverse
1663 Liberty Drive
Bloomington, IN 47403
www.iuniverse.com
1-800-Authors (1-800-288-4677)

ISBN: 978-1-4620-3227-3 (sc)

Printed in the United States of America

iUniverse rev. date: 07/15/2011

ACKNOWLEDGEMENTS

My deep gratitude for the generosity, empathy and tolerance for reading and viewing photos therein, and for all the photographers albeit bulk of the photos were taken by me, some by my mother and other bystanders also volunteered and offered to take photos on my behalf. I thank in advance for all the countless Americans and other residents and visitors who are somehow featured in photos in this book for these are for the sake of teaching and building tolerance in USA and not intended to misrepresent those depicted in certain photos and so in this sense, the entire book can be categorized as a documentary writing and photos.

Thank you all and God bless you.

Dorothy Myung-Soo Hong
New York
April 2011

Having Problems and Issues means we are alive and we want to improve quality of life.

Koreans come to America because of welcome signs from US government agencies abroad and attractive commercials and because Koreans have the means to purchase at least the plane tickets and get by at least a couple of months without assistance. Most importantly, under immigration laws they realize Korean immigrants will have been able to fill in sector noted with or most pronounced by the shortage of labor with their schooling and experience in scientific, health, artistic, ministry and other enterprising and entrepreneur joint venture opportunities, such as OEM or IP licensing to promote more cross-border transactions. Historically, most Koreans have been friendly or nonchalant to Europeans and Americans visiting Korea so naturally they expect similar reciprocity in treatments.

Generally, like any other American citizen, Koreans who immigrate to the US look for First Amendment rights that are more broad and complex and tolerant and thereby affording latitude in one's actions and thoughts and at the same time giving the impression of cold, brutal and impersonal society where things are so much in flux that even a loud mouth's constant motion of utterance in an effort to exercise his free speech to the fullest to make his voice heard to people near and far just adds up to a mere element of constant motion of acceptable and expected and foreseen formula results such that in the competition of ideas, in terms of both thoughts, speech and conducts things will fall and settle into its proper place and perspective or are dismissed or overlooked. A response even a negative reaction is better than a total taciturn where people in this category of political orientation considers you insignificant and invisible and many times they simply say, "I can't hear you," "I didn't see that," or "Sorry, I forgot but you'll have to wait a little longer." Or else other knee jerk reaction fielded by prejudice and racism is usually, "Get rid of it" or "Raped and murder that uppity one in quick and dirty way," or "Let's do a deal and leave them out on the street or leave them in our stomach until expulsion and down into toilet and into sewage system." I think when a statesman worries about his constituents and ctizens and says "I don't want to be in a soup," he normally means he wants to assure job security for all citizens who want to work to reduce unemployment rate and take measures in making sure everybody is fed so that citizens do not go hungry at night before going to sleep. Ergo he means the noble spirit of civil servant or public service life of serving and working for others. "Whom do you work for?" Even a sole proprietor has an answer and so does an adoptee or sponsored beneficiary and better yet a hanger-on or a guest. We all chip in and do our part. We all work for somebody, some company, some organization, that is to say in contractual relationship engaging in hopefully lawful activities at all stages. Hopefully, where work environment is cordial and devoid of fear of hostile work environment with screams and shouts of racial slurs for even a slight inadvertent oversight by unwitting minority or newcomer.

My theory is 95% of people meaning American population outside my heritage can be characterized as dictionary definition of racist practicing racism. That is, they are racist, they think of their own race only, weigh judgment or make assessment that tends to favor their own race and to the detriment of other races. Some people believe and have compelling reason to engage in quick and immediate action and measure to assure one race stays atop, recognized as superior and majority in all avenue at all cost at all time in any and all means to achieve this end to feel powerful and superior. And this becomes all time consuming for some with every moment intrusive thought and obsessive thought triggering him to seize the racist moment and savor it and compulsively behaves so as to even condone evil and wicked conducts that using common sense and reading Moses' Ten Commandments and not necessarily having knowledge of esoteric proviso of certain legal code would shed light. To do otherwise is simply be a loser, disrupt status quo and really for other minority members to be "pushing the envelope and asking for it," and the only option for a racist is then in the name of dispensing knowledge to enable what racists deem "psychotic and uppity minority" to cope and gain proper perspective and reality so as not to make "that kind of accidental mistake," next time because whites are important and non-whites are not, kind of mind set.

Unfortunately many times these kinds of racists conducts entail fatality, illness, casualty, kidnapping, bombing and sometimes segregation with torture and unspeakable sex crimes so as to shut the mouths of victims or conveniently, such atrocities are not broadcasted because these are unaccounted for population or dead without dead certificates. An example of American groups indulging in these criminal activities preying on newcomers with bank accounts are Hazzebollah and other hate groups categorized under Patriot Groups. The reason for the long kept secret is after all, decent people don't talk about money lost or failing health or for that matter that any events in their personal life adversely affecting their dignity to strangers, well not even to relatives or family members of friends. Koreans want to be in a picture perfect integrated professional setting where everything seems smooth sailing with no room for discord or airing issues or problems. This is their idea of harmony, community living and Korean pride.

Why would any findings of terror related corpse/body part(s) in any neighborhood, arson or bone breaking, skin lesion battery, other intrusive invasive measure to body or snow-boarding for that matter serve as a positive reinforcement that white people are benevolent ruling class who are able to grasp and assess degree of pain and persecution suffered by discreet minority members and these white at the same time would seem attractive and sometimes so irresistibly sexy that white sigh and say, "We can't work! We're sexy, we're white," or "Asian chick just passed by 7 feet away on the same street so my date with my heartthrob is totally ruined because I know the Asian is a clinging vine."

I remember a food fight with a fellow WASP male student long time ago after his snickering that I worked on suicide and gay rights along with Affirmative Action programs while active in student government in school. After a shouting match, we sat down and discussed the matter in the Dean's office. The associate dean was kind enough to let usage of the conference room and iron out things there and mend the seam. My fellow white classmate said, "My racism is better than yours because it was thoughtless and accidental and it came naturally while you really had to think deeply and for a long time with chocolate cake and coffee breaks to come to the conclusion that it was a manifestation of racism," or something like that. My memory is rather foggy but people have been commenting about my caffeine consumption to avoid my sleeping through it all.

Then, there are other types of work colleagues who say "Good morning," with bright big smile, and actually delegate work or work together on projects or deals together. But unbeknownst to a hard working minority member thinking his talent is recognized in an integrated work force, some of his white peers have "Dr. Jekyll and Mr. Hyde," psycho-profile where they release and vent what they consider outrage that minorities are literally crawling all over them, seeping their blood and stepping all over them soon setting themselves for the superior, manager positions pushing them out and below. White's effort to eradicate and discredit racial remnants of slavery days and Chinese dynastic days so that recognized author, inventor, painter would be accorded credits and fair compensation to these Dr. Jekyll and Mr. Hyde group of people are unthinkable and threatening. Why stealing and killing front liner Asian enthusiasts is an easy living for fine living some have proved.

How does tyrannized, isolated and terrorized minority member respond this kind of milieu? Does he go along at all cost, remaining silent, acquiescing to everything, even acting like a sycophant, patsy or co-conspirator in an accessory manner? Does he fight back, call attention to management or law enforcement or litigate or prosecute the matter or even arbitrate or discuss in a meeting? Does he behave in a robotic machine-like rigidity, remaining totally silent, wooden and inscrutable and everything being swept under the rug so as not to embarrass anyone and then the "Big Bang" time with everything destroyed and everyone betrayed and the minority member is nowhere to be found because he left town and changed his identity?

There is a fundamental hurdle in various groups and propensity of each to indulge in certain predictable activities. Easy living, easy thinking and easy way only and easy things to do and easy action to feel good and not feel so much taxed and furious.

Below is a chart from traditional Korean philosophy translated to accepted popular customs:

Coins	Traditional Ideas	Thematic Components: Ideational Orientation	Pursuits and Needs, Emotional Disposition	Design Motif Symbols
	<u>Nature and Man</u>	Nature & the Cosmos are one	Awe and fear of nature	Celestial bodies (the sun, moon, and stars)
		Nature is the sovereign force over all things	Love of nature	T'aeguk
		Nature, the life giver, governs human life with its laws	Sense of security from nature worship	Mountain
		Nature Changes, but is eternal and its power infinite	Plea for nature's blessings	Circle
		Nature is both benevolent and malevolent	Humble dependency upon nature	Heavenly twin
		Man is a part of Nature		
	<u>Life and Death</u>	Life is given	Fear of violent death	Celestial bodies; life granting & life regulating stars
		Life is short	Love of well-ordered life	
		Life continues after death	Desire for longevity & acceptance of natural death [lotus]	Sip changsaeng (10 long-life objects)
		Life and be perpetuated through sons		
		Human souls and spirits survive death	Belief in reincarnation and salvation	Gourd
		Death is a part of life, not a destructive force. With death a new but unknown life begins	Value of family, many sons & ancestor worship. Fear of uncertainty of the afterlife	

Coins	Traditional Ideas	Thematic Components: Ideational Orientation	Pursuits and Needs, Emotional Disposition	Design Motif Symbols
	Human Relationship	Basic moral principles exist to regulate human relationships. All human relations are vertical / horizontal	Love of family	P'algwae-eight trigrams
		Rules governing family relationships are basic to all other relationships	Dependency on the protective superior	Diamond heart
		Human relationships are changeable and impermanent	Desire for appeasement to reduce tension	
		Wisdom is the key to the maintenance of meaningful relationship	Values of humility, gentleness, respectfulness, and modesty	
			Desire for true friendship based on trust	
			Fear of transient relationships. Value of fidelity and constancy. Sense of shame in human conflict.	
	Wealth	Wealth is bestowed	Desire for wealth	Celestial bodies
		Wealth depends on luck and chance	Fear of poverty	Precious objects (metals and stones)
		Wealth is power	Belief in luck	Sea
		Wealth is to be displayed	Dependency of wealth	
		Wealth equals nobility	Fatalistic attitude toward wealth	
		Wealth should be preserved	Wealth is not the result of labor	
		Wealth means possession of precious objects	Passive envy for the wealthy	

Coins	Traditional Ideas	Thematic Components: Ideational Orientation	Pursuits and Needs, Emotional Disposition	Design Motif Symbols
	Body & Mind	Body elements have their counterparts in nature	Love of body as part of nature	Earth
		Strong body means equilibrium between various elements	Desire for health, for longevity	Water
		Each body part interacts with other body parts	Fear of sickness	Fire
		Health equals longevity & natural death	High value on curative (medicinal) objects	Wind
		Elements in nature have curative effects	Belief in moderation	Bat
		Mind (heart, soul, spirit) dwells in body. Mind is regulated by body & vice versa. Death takes mind out of the body.	Belief in survival of mind after death. Wish for long life of heath and peace.	Weight

Source: The Korean National Commission for UNESCO 1983 ISBN 0-89209-018-9, p.254 The Five Blessings and Koreans Coin Charms

Compare with the chart below which is a Westernized interpretation of Biblical Virtues Americans espouse as a matter of their Christian practice:

Virtue	Biblical quote	Bible text source
Salvation	Lord, let salvation spring up within my children that they may obtain the salvation that is in Christ Jesus, with eternal glory.	Is. 45:8, 2Tim. 2:10
Growth in grace	I pray that my children may grow in the grace and knowledge of our Lord and Savior Jesus Christ.	2Pet. 3:18
Love	Grant, Lord, that my children may learn to live a life of love, through the Spirit who dwells in them	Gal. 5:25, Eph. 5:2
Honesty and integrity	May integrity and honesty be their virtue and their protection	Ps. 25:21
Self-control	Father, help my children not to be like many others around them, but let them be alert and self-controlled in all they do.	1Thes. 5:6
Love for God's Word	May my children grow to find Your Word more precious than much pure gold and sweeter than honey from the comb.	Ps. 19:10
Justice	God, help my children grow to love justice as You do and act justly in all they do.	Ps. 11:7, Mic. 6:8
Mercy	May my children always be merciful, just as their Father is merciful.	Lk. 6:36
Respect (for self, others, authority)	Father, grant that my children may show proper respect to everyone, as your Word commands.	1Pet. 2:17
Biblical self-esteem	Help, my children develop a strong self-esteem that is rooted in the realization that they are God's workmanship, created in Christ Jesus.	Eph. 2:10
Faithfulness	Lt love and faithful never leave my children, but bind these twin virtues around their necks and write them on the tablet of their hearts.	Prov. 3:3
Courage	May my children always be strong and courageous in their character and in their actions.	Dt. 31:6

Virtue	Biblical quote	Bible text source
Purity	Create in them a pure heart, O God, and let that purity of heart be shown in their actions.	Ps. 51:10
Kindness	Lord, may my children always try to be kind to each other and to everyone else.	1Thess. 5:15
Generosity	Grant that my children may be generous and willing to share, and so lay up treasure for themselves as a firm foundation for the coming age.	1Tim. 6:18-19
Peace-loving	Father, let my children make every effort to do what leads to peace.	Rom. 14-19
Joy	May my children be filled with the joy given by the Holy Spirit	1Thess. 1:6
Perseverance	Lord, teach my children perseverance in all they do, and help them especially to run with perseverance the race marked out for them.	Heb. 12:1
Humility	God, please cultivate in my children the ability to show true humility toward all.	Titus 3:2
Compassion	Lord, please clothe my children with the virtue of compassion.	Col. 3:12
Responsibility	Grant that my children may learn responsibility, for each one should carry his own load.	Gal. 6:5
Contentment	Father, teach my children the secret of being content in any and every situation, through Him who gives them strength.	Phil. 4:12-13
Faith	I pray that faith will find root and grow in my children's hearts, that by faith they may gain what has been promised to them.	Lk. 17:5-6, Heb. 11:1-40
A servant's heart	God, please help my children develop servant's hearts, which they may serve wholeheartedly, as if they were serving the Lord, not men.	Col. 3:23
Hope	May the God of hope grant that my children may overflow with hope and hopefulness by the power of the Holy Spirit.	Ro. 15:13
Willingness and ability to work	Teach my children, Lord, to value work and to work at it with all their hearts, as working for the Lord, not to men.	Col. 3:23

Dorothy M. Hong

Virtue	Biblical quote	Bible text source
Passion for God	Lord, please instill in my children a soul that followed hard after thee, one that clings passionately to you.	Ps. 63:8: KJV
Self-discipline	Father, I pray that my children may acquire a disciplined and prudent life, doing what is right and just and fair.	Prov. 1:3
Prayerfulness	Grant, Lord, that my children's lives may be marked by prayerfulness, which they may learn to pray in the Spirit on all occasions with all kinds of prayers and requests.	Eph. :18
Gratitude	Help my children to live lives that are always overflowing with thankfulness and always giving thanks to God the Father for everything, in the name of our Lord Jesus Christ.	Eph. 5:20, Col. 2:7
A heart of mission	Lord, please help my children to develop a desire to see your glory declared among the nations, your marvelous deeds among all peoples.	Ps. 96:3

Source: Biblical Virtues to pray for your kids by Bob Hostetler (Excerpted from Pray! Magazine issue #4 (© 1998 Bob Hostetler) www.praymag.com. ISBN# 1576839001

Comments and observations

Just from comparing these two charts above we can immediately sense obstacles Koreans will have confronted in integrating, interacting and dealing with Americans, most notably white Americans from Europe. There is so much premium in Buddhism for tranquility and orderliness between fellow citizens and with superiors that trumps any activity or movement guided by faith and fueled by hope because these movements and progress may imply competition which may imply rivalry and hostility, discussion, arguments, disagreements which may lead to disclosure of certain facts and setting aside of time, sometimes waste of time and most notably any progress or movement being perceived as threat to status quo not limited to ostensible meaning accorded such as law and order but pointing to fragility and corruptibility of power and any shift of power.

Christian virtues do not hide that we mortals are sinners and may head for destruction of grand scale if left unchecked by moral, mental, emotional, spiritual disciplines that well meaning Christian practice demands. Christian practice puts great premium on action which ought to be monitored and tapered and in moderation, but perspiration, labor and earnestness guided by faith are presumed to be favored by God. Action and passion so integral to well heeled functionality of democracy and capitalism rooted in equality, liberty and justice under God may appear at first glance bothersome and laborious to Koreans especially when dealing with bullying and prejudiced white Americans who are also easily provoked into retaliatory measures or worst yet revert them to inaction and no correspondence and ties leading to zero interaction and transaction. Creation, progress, movement in orderly and tranquil manner is not only counter-intuitive to human nature but it is also against the law of nature and order.

Remember with passage of time each week, rooms get messier unless we exert energy and make effort to clean.

Persistent Program Scenarios:

1. In the course of employment/business consideration manager asks about Korean perspective candidate. Korean who's never been afforded an opportunity to speak talks about all kinds of things flaunting his/her personal knowledge and sometimes makes up story any way in an effort to project into the mind of employer who has been hostile to Korean employee and his ethnic origin.

2. A fellow Korean (A) ethnic origin is perceived as having a bigger slice of pie or has positioned him in most enviable, venerable establishment where minorities are unheard of. Here the danger of outsider Korean is that of obsession, i.e. thinking about Korean(A) is annoying, nuisance fueled by jealousy and desire to protect Korean(A) out of pride) and stepping in his shoes and fantasizing outsider to feel connected with this Korean (A) by groping for any gossip or inversely getting unwanted telephones about Korean (A) prompting and inciting outsider to act in anti-social manner adversely impacting Koreans as a whole.

3. A Korean (B) is afforded an opportunity of wealth, power and secrecy but later learned that their activities entailed illegal conducts often harming Koreans and Korea but Korean (B) feels special, tickled, thrilled and energized that he is able to hurt other people the way he was hurt and feels comforted, secure and little responsibility because his harmful conducts will have been executed at the request of people Korean (B) deems powerful, attractive and influential, not to mention fear that these whites instill.

4. While some people are as good as dead and are silent so as not to embarrass victims or perpetrators others fret and complain. What is a course of action a Korean lost in sea of white crowd can do to protect his interest, rights, family and safety of others near him.

5. One's sister/mother/girl friend or close colleague was humiliated, harassed or ravaged. How do we turn away from irresponsible and cowardly behavior out of dread and fear of white admonishment and retaliatory measures and stand up to protect theses victims

to restore equilibrium in Korean family, social, community, male/female dynamics structures and at the same time let white Americans know that their illegal, irresponsible, criminal, depraved heart misconducts, recklessness and carelessness coupled with brutality will not be tolerated as a way of American life. How else to explain the birth of USA as a new nation?

6. How do Koreans go about accepting our own sense of aesthetics and usual business course of dealings and lawful normal contracts when outsiders demand inordinate attention, esteem and even our assets and resources at the risk of loss of property and life let alone humiliation from losing face by Korean.

7. How do we go about asserting our place and rights, birth rights, God given rights, natural rights, Constitutional rights, when we sense immediately incompatibility and imbalance in physical rigor, wealth of resources and unfathomable wealth where Koreans do not have access but Koreans come to realize later that some of these white Americans have plundered, racketeered or otherwise brain washed us from massive marketing and media and publication efforts. How can we make smart, cost effective choice and those that are absolutely necessary which white Americans may not inform us in timely manner.

8. How do we disagree or make them aware of lack of our willful consent or displeasure which would ultimately enable white Americans to make rational decisions and do not waste their life on cover ups, conspiracy, corruption and erroneous facts, fallacy or lies.

9. Sometimes people say, "You don't fit in," when these statements show intent to make us not fit in and uttered ones may have uttered out of their own insecure sense of fitting in or projecting on to the few who speak out loud racial epithets, curse, fighting words, provocation to overwhelm disinterested and other hostile white Americans in a spirit of cohesive and comforting team-man ship fueled by hysteria of a few who must feel superior and sexier at all time, at all cost in all avenue thinking that he is voicing the concerns of the entire white nation with hate talk and misconducts.

10. How do we teach modesty to non-Koreans who then feel outraged that they have been snubbed and belittled and cry wolf to all these professional people at the risk of exposing something private and sacred to instill a new sense of cohesion and inclusion among whites using glues made of butchered, fried and pulverized innocent, high achieving, law abiding and unknowing Korean. Corollary to this is does getting sexed by Blacks add "professionalism" to credentials?

I am also attaching my Google Blogger to add to this theme to shed light on some of misgivings blacks and whites have about Asians' "decision points" to integrate, sometimes pioneer and other times making effort to party together and network together with those they deem out group. One need not exercise every single rights and privileges but on the other hand exercising rights and privileges as US citizens, residents and visitors should not have to endure penalty of grand scale and cruel and unusual punishment.

I remember once making a faux pas when I felt a microphone pointing to a seat in front of me where a man sat in front of me unaware that I said aloud a greeting exchange words when microphone was facing his butt. But seriously, I meant no ill feeling. It was a natural inclination, an accidental, involuntary gesture. On that note, here is a clip from my Google blogger.

Follow   Share   Report Abuse   Next Blog»   dmshong@gmail.com   New Post   Design   Sign Out

Dorothy Hong's Blogger

Monday, December 13, 2010

Providing life necessities, safety and proper rest and ethical work are good reasons and incentives to acquiece and/or enter into contract to accept as such providers as superior protector, but some are lured, instead, by the opportunity to associate and be part of secretive, exclusive rich, famous and powerful ruling people/race/class/caste promising the same with undying sacrifice and fidality in return to such a scam schemer which is sometimes confused as superior protector.

Posted by DorothyMHongBlogger at 7:14 AM 0 comments

Monday, July 19, 2010

Westchester County neighborhood

I live about 1/2 hr ride from Harlem Line to Grand Central and 1/2 hr ride from New Haven Line to Stamford. The community in which I live is pretty much homogenous lot vis-a-vis my own area of work, hobby and religion. Yet people ask me, "What's it like," because, I suppose, I am an Asian immigrant. Well, I've been too busy keeping a roof over my head, making sure I eat right and stay warm in winter and cool in summer and this pretty much becomes all consuming task aside from a few solitary moments I set aside for reading, prayer, rest and keeping up with bill payments. There are some others, though, who are similarly situated as I am and who make tremendous strides, sacrifices and inroads with regard to community activities/services/interactions and so they probabaly have more shindigs and travel plans together of which I may not be aware. Most of the year end parties I've had were primarily with Korean immigrants. I know some Ivy Leaguers who come out of school who concede that inbreeding is just not convenient when you have eyes focused on financial success and fame in the mainstream America. In general, however, most Korean parents would concede, instead, that Korean immigrant success portrait depends on having their offsprings marry other Koreans in America and having their progeny look similar in coating as those Korean ancestors upon their port of entry via immigration beacuse it does not take very many generations of interbreeding to make Koreans look totally Caucasian, etc. For this reason, I think that as Korean immigrant population exceeds 5,000 in Southern Westchester County that its community consider Cultural or Ethnic Associations primarily for Koreans, separate from Korean churches because American pop culture does not seem to afford Dabang leisure gathering so Korean residents either end up driving around to shop or end up joining

Blog Archive

About Me

DorothyMHongBlogger

Teachers who influenced Dorothy are Lee, Un Woo, her private art tutor, Peter Katzenstein and Karen Brazell from Cornell and Paul Shechtman and Julius L. Chambers from Penn Law. Dorothy Hong is the direct descendant of Mal Soo Shin, a younger brother of Sook Joo Shin, the lead scholar/Yangban who invented Hangul during Yi dynasty and the great-grand daughter of Jin Hong, a lawyer from Yangban family and independence movement leader during Japanese Occupation Period and grand niece of Tae Ah Yu, a former Ambassador to Japan.

View my complete profile

Dorothy M. Hong

Dorothy Hong's Blogger

Monday, December 13, 2010

Providing life necessities, safety and proper rest and ethical work are good reasons and incentives to acquiece and/or enter into contract to accept as such providers as superior protector, but some are lured, instead, by the opportunity to associate and be part of secretive, exclusive rich, famous and powerful ruling people/race/class/caste promising the same with undying sacrifice and fidality in return to such a scam schemer which is sometimes confused as superior protector.

Posted by DorothyMHongBlogger at 7:14 AM 0 comments

Monday, July 19, 2010

Westchester County neighborhood

I live about 1/2 hr ride from Harlem Line to Grand Central and 1/2 hr ride from New Haven Line to Stamford. The community in which I live is pretty much homogenous lot vis-a-vis my own area of work, hobby and religion. Yet people ask me, "What's it like," because, I suppose, I am an Asian immigrant. Well, I've been too busy keeping a roof over my head, making sure I eat right and stay warm in winter and cool in summer and this pretty much becomes all consuming task aside from a few solitary moments I set aside for reading, prayer, rest and keeping up with bill payments. There are some others, though, who are similarly situated as I am and who make tremendous strides, sacrifices and inroads with regard to community activities/services/interactions and so they probabaly have more shindigs and travel plans together of which I may not be aware. Most of the year end parties I've had were primarily with Korean immigrants. I know some Ivy Leaguers who come out of school who concede that inbreeding is just not convenient when you have eyes focused on financial success and fame in the mainstream America. In general, however, most Korean parents would concede, instead, that Korean immigrant success portrait depends on having their offsprings marry other Koreans in America and having their progeny look similar in coating as those Korean ancestors upon their port of entry via immigration beacuse it does not take very many generations of interbreeding to make Koreans look totally Caucasion, etc. For this reason, I think that as Korean immigrant population exceeds 5,000 in Southern Westchester County that its community consider Cultural or Ethnic Associations primarily for Koreans, separate from Korean churches because American pop culture does not seem to afford Dabang leisure gathering so Korean residents either end up driving around to shop or end up joining

Followers

Follow   0
with Google Friend Connect

There are no followers yet
Be the first!

Already a member? Sign in

Blog Archive

▼ 2010 (5)
  ▼ December (1)
    Providing life necessities, safety and blogger rest...
  ► July (1)
  ► May (1)
  ► April (2)

About Me

DorothyMHongBlogger

Teachers who influenced Dorothy are Lee, Un Woo, her private art tutor, Peter Katzenstein and Karen Brazell from Cornell and Paul Shechtman and Julius L. Chambers from Penn Law. Dorothy Hong is the direct descendant of Mal Joo Shin, a younger brother of Sosk Joo Shin, the lead scholar/Yangban who invented Hangui during Yi dynasty and the great-grand daughter of Jin Hong, a lawyer and independence movement leader during Japanese Occupation Period and grand-niece of Tae Ah Yu, a former Ambassador to Japan.

View my complete profile

Source: Blog: Dorothy Hong's Blogger
Link: http://dorothymhongblogger.blogspot.com/2010/12/providing-life-necessities-safety-and.html

According to the current census, Southern Westchester, New York enjoys a diverse population of about 5% Asian, 13% blacks, 22% Hispanics and less than 1% Native Americans and the rest Caucasians. I remember going to Wilmington, Delaware once and passing by beautiful old mansion section of a certain Brandywine neighborhood. The taxi driver told me, "These are beautiful homes of successful people but they don't have children," which reminds me of Sir Thomas More's statement to his daughter during his final days when he said in an under one breath, "Life, death."

Other Terrorist Concerns Requiring Focus and Attention

Although al-Qa'ida is our strategic as well as tactical CT priority, other designated terrorist organizations pose a significant threat to U.S. strategic interests. Hizballah, HAMAS, and the Revolutionary Armed Forces of Colombia (FARC) remain opposed to aspects of U.S. foreign policy and pose significant threats to U.S. strategic interests as regional destabilizers and as threats to our citizens, facilities, and allies worldwide. Even when their terrorist efforts are not directed at the United States, a successful terrorist operation by one of these groups in and around the key regional fault lines in which they operate increases the likelihood of regional conflict. We remain committed to understanding the intention and capabilities of these groups, as well as working with our partners to disrupt terrorist operations and related activities that threaten regional and international security and threaten our national security objectives. In addition to the threats posed by al-Qa'ida and its affiliates and adherents, U.S. citizens and interests are at times threatened by other violent groups within the Homeland and across the globe. We will remain vigilant to these threats and regularly advise the American people of local risks.

Iran and Syria remain active sponsors of terrorism, and we remain committed to opposing the support these state sponsors provide to groups pursuing terrorist attacks to undermine regional stability.

Source: LinkedIn presentation slides of US Oval Office issued on June 2011 on "National Strategy for Counterterrorism ("CT")"

Asian/Korean Studies and Meetings

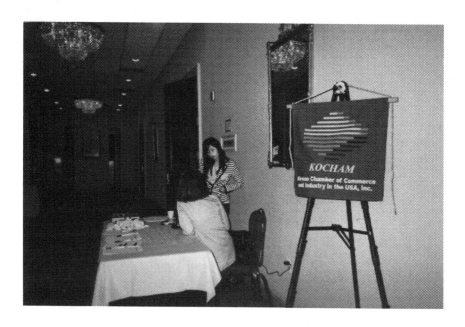

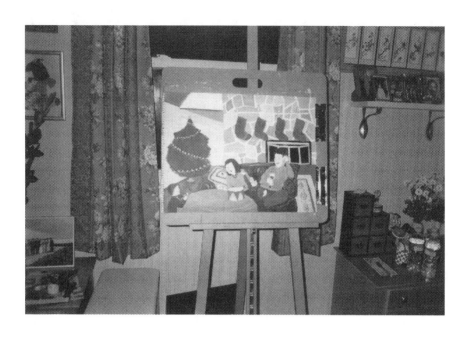

Epilogue

Ethics in publication of narration which is in accord with evidentiary ruling of hearsay exception of present sense impression as being reliable to the extent it is admissible in court rooms before judge would lead us to believe that George W. Bush's account of his eight years in White House serving two terms of US Presidency is more accurate and reliable than Neville Chamberlain's biography published in 2006, that is fifty six years after his passing away in 1940. Yet in each final chapter of each book, each author asks the reader pointedly, "What is the verdict," based on reader's reading comprehension of the world leader described therein who made pivotal quick personal decisions in the spirit of appeasement of important allies for the sake of "correct" foreign policy and for domestic stability to reduce chance of recession or rising unemployment rate.

I know War briefly gives a false and urgent sense of unity and team spirit in an otherwise brutal, catty and mean society filled with inequities and injustices that tend to create chasms between classes, education levels, regions and political orientations.

How did Bush administration deal with Arabs who wanted to concede and play "game" for fun in the name of developing true spirituality and harmony with ecosystem for the sake of worshiping their God vis-à-vis discriminations against Semitic race and Aryan bastards in Asia by destroying key venues? How did the British Prime Minister Neville Chamberlain work so closely with Adolf Hitler knowing that provoking Germany is like committing suicide while dealing with French and Turks alone cannot bring peace in Mediterranean region or with Balkans but at least that was the strategy for the English stand point leaving aside Japan for English to work with alone in the end.

Isn't the real issue a superficial standard that men set certain idealized criteria for beauty and many concede that beauty is associated with virtue, purity, propertied high class dame and almost always from mainline real McCoy well respected well heeled patrician family with large family libraries and who almost always return library books to the Public Libraries every book they borrow. It is ridiculous to say honoring woman of this milieu at even a false hint of assault by an achieving alien while back office financiers are making billions with the help of collusion with the same dame all for the sake of saving some Saxon lord pagan of bygone days who is lost in China, for argument sake. The enlightened establishments seem to have gotten all worked up for nothing and their rationale and reason for actions may in the end be meaningless and feel defeated by their own prejudices designed to protect the innocent victims whom in fact these pointy politicians have been persecuting.

This is racism in a tall rhetorical words and politics maneuvering to engage everyone in it to give the kind of momentum of winning, let's say, Lotto. If you roll your dice right and have your pinky fall on the right numbers on the cell phone, for argument sake, you may just be the next billionaire.

Arabs would probably have the best knowledge of integrated Jews, their native homeland neighbors. Jews would probably have the best network to determine who in fact are soliciting their help for illegal purpose for the sake of elevating WASP Dom with the promise that Jews would inherit America on an equal footing as WASPS dating back to Puritan days in terms of power, wealth and establishment. Status quo no longer means law and order.

America, on the other hand, sees its society as a rat race and doggy dog world relishing at the thought of Orientalizing victim class or race or community. Yet unless you're stupid or irrationally smug, you have to keep in mind "movement with intelligence." I suppose you can't expect others to forgive you just because you harbor vindication yourself, but at times you're at luck because either people don't know, don't care or overlook unessential element of their own life and livelihood. Bravery and heroism still exist and some actually turn away from their family, friends, their peers and the race in which he belongs to side with God, the truth and justice after a long period of earning grace by slowing down and of course because quite simply he didn't have all the pieces of puzzles together.

Maybe so that they can sleep at night without worrying themselves, eating themselves out and spending the rest of their lives to live up to the upkeep that they managed to create for themselves starting from shady practice that they now want to cover up. Better yet some culprits yearn, "Well, everybody's doing it and so therefore it is America's favorite past time."

Bible's Proverbs, Roman and Philippians would have answer to these puzzle pieces God laid out for us but most citizens would rather marry, have children, rear family, engage in livelihood in accord with their education investment and continue civilization even though they may silently acknowledge corruption at the highest level.

Who determines national interest and does it have to be an alien influx demanding political reform that signals national security.

My verdict is as follows: sometimes you have to purchase a new disk driver and start from fresh Operating System after having lost all your saved work and programs in the "c" drive so that your computer can work again. But this is not always necessary when you can afford a new and improved computer. Ergo, there is no such thing as the "righteous and correct" foreign policy, but we all know war is hell and "fight and make up" is an old cliché that may not work in an inter-racial context.

The Rev. Martin Luther King Jr's grand spiritual and kind gesture to welcome and open the flood gate of sinners to enter and integrate amongst each other at homes and offices so that greatest talents and goals may be achieved while God is watching us and thereby affording everyone an opportunity to study, research, develop friendship, worship and sit next to each other at cafeteria or dine at the same restaurant regardless of race but bound by instead by shared value, talent, interest and trait are so magnanimous for me to even entertain the possibility and probability of success, peace and harmony that I feel petty and small next to this preacher and peacemaker like Dr. Martin Luther King Jr.

During childhood I grew up with a fabled picture book about a shivering snake needing a shelter beseeching to a farmer who had a long day of labor and toil. The farmer sympathizes with the snake and out of kindness extends invitation to his home. But as soon as the snake is warmed up he wags and plays with his long sharp tongue and then starts to attack farmer's children whom snake considers yummy food. Farmer, to protect himself and his family, kills the snake.

But this is not to give up on integration, diversity, liberty and affording minority rights to air and have them articulate new, exciting and unexpected as well as disagreeable and different perspectives. In reality, however, we often see silence or chiming in from the minority sector. Not allowing even subversive minority group to exercise First Amendment rights of free speech is de facto making this country a Godless savage state, where citizens may be obsessed with winning, being rich and powerful. These worshippers of materialism take their frustration out on those who seem less formidable, powerless and who are resigned from any retaliatory measures out of fear, terror and oppression and tyranny of majority. Some people view silence as agreement or acquiescence and so it's easy cake walk but remember the old saying that some dogs bark while others bite.

For me the following formula ought to be workable in USA, a land of democracy and capitalism where soon or later one will come to realize and appreciate one's limitations and mistakes and recognize need to take a break and rest and seek God. As for me it doesn't matter that I work the whole day at the exclusion of others just for the sake of maximum wage. From God's point of view, as Jesus pointed out in his parable, it's more important that work gets finished even by hiring a last minute laborer for one hour at the same wage as me who toiled the whole day.

So therefore, work ethics, proper rest, good work to the extent we can do them and earning grace by slowing down, taking time out for self-reflection, repentance, confession, self-restraint and self-regulation. That is to say, let things be and let nature take its course without meddling to intentionally determine outcomes.

Here is a lyric to a song I just wrote inspired by looking at the cloudless blue sky after reading Nietzsche at my leisure.

Lyrics to Jesus was our sacrifice to lift our sins and burdens and follow his teachings

by Dorothy Myung-Soo Hong

I love my heritage, I love my brothers, I love my family and friends and neighbors.
I love the servants, I love the teachers, I love the governors, and I love the movie stars, the cooks, the police officers and the waiters.

I want to be close to Jesus Christ, I want to fly to see the heaven, I want to dive and swim to feel like Jesus walking on ocean with my fervant faith

I love you Jesus, I love you Jesus. You saved me from loneliness and despair. I love you Jesus you saved me from my invisible presence and unspeakable history.

You put a dignity and a melody to screams and shouts. You saved a sinner like me and transformed my wicked mind to decency in conduct and purity in thought

I remember Jesus in each communion. His bread his body and his wine his blood. I remember Jesus and his last supper. His love and kindness and his foresight and vision.

Repeat:
I want to be a sacrifice like Jesus sacrificed for humankind.

I want to be a sacrifice like Jesus cleared our sins.

I want to be a sacrifice like Jesus shed us grace.

I want to be a sacrifice to know the righteous.

I want to be a sacrifice to save the wickedness, to save the homeless, to save the penniless and those without parents and without trust funds.

I want to be a sacrifice to save the blind and deaf, to save the deformed and the lepers and the confused souls
I want to be a sacrifice to save and heal the psychosis and sickness.

I want to be a sacrifice so people can be in harmony, whether beauty or savage, whether small or large, whether smart or dull or rich or poor.

I want to be a sacrifice! Please Jesus hear my prayer.
Please Jesus come to our gathering if not so let me be, be close to Jesus.

I'd like to end and compare with a translation of Korean hymn by Young Taek Jung (1894-1968) translated by John T. Underwood, 1988

All Year in Our Home the Spring Breezes Blow

Verse 3 – Korean English Hymnal

One house-hold, working till all work is done, Morning and evening in love and good cheer.

One table, with food and drink shared as one. This is our Garden of Eden right here!

How we thank Him Immanuel! Our home His, His to serve Christ always!

How we thank Him, Immanuel! Such joy and blessedness, day upon day.

- Korean -English Hymnal
Korean Hymnal Society, Seoul, Korea, Published by:

Christian Literature Society, Seoul, Korea, 1984

Homeland Security

Appendix (Reference) 2 pages from
Homeland Security DHS Yearbook of
Immigration Statistics 2010

Yearbook of Immigration Statistics: 2010
Immigrants

Table #	Title
Table 1	Persons Obtaining Legal Permanent Resident Status: Fiscal Years 1820 to 2010 *(XLS, 29 KB)*
Table 2	Persons Obtaining Legal Permanent Resident Status by Region and Selected Country of Last Residence: Fiscal Years 1820 to 2010 *(XLS, 27 KB)*
Table 3	Persons Obtaining Legal Permanent Resident Status by Region and Country of Birth: Fiscal Years 2001 to 2010 *(XLS, 29 KB)*
Table 4	Persons Obtaining Legal Permanent Resident Status by State or Territory of Residence: Fiscal Years 2001 to 2010 *(XLS, 16 KB)*
Table 5	Persons Obtaining Legal Permanent Resident Status by Core Based Statistical Area (CBSA) of Residence: Fiscal Years 2001 to 2010 *(XLS, 40 KB)*
Table 6	Persons Obtaining Legal Permanent Resident Status by Type and Major Class of Admission: Fiscal Years 2001 to 2010 *(XLS, 41 KB)*
Table 7	Persons Obtaining Legal Permanent Resident Status by Type and Detailed Class of Admission: Fiscal Year 2010 *(XLS, 31 KB)*
Table 8	Persons Obtaining Legal Permanent Resident Status by Gender, Age, Marital Status, and Occupation: Fiscal Year 2010 *(XLS, 14 KB)*
Table 9	Persons Obtaining Legal Permanent Resident Status by Broad Class of Admission and Selected Demographic Characteristics: Fiscal Year 2010 *(XLS, 15 KB)*
Table 10	Persons Obtaining Legal Permanent Resident Status by Broad Class of Admission and Region and Country of Birth: Fiscal Year 2010 *(XLS, 25 KB)*
Table 11	Persons Obtaining Legal Permanent Resident Status by Broad Class of Admission and Region and Country of Last Residence: Fiscal Year 2010 *(XLS, 25 KB)*
Table 12	Immigrant Orphans Adopted by U.S. Citizens by Gender, Age, and Region and Country of Birth: Fiscal Year 2010 *(XLS, 15 KB)*

Supplemental Tables

Table #	Title
Supplemental Table 1	Persons Obtaining Legal Permanent Resident Status by State or Territory of Residence and Region and Country of Birth: Fiscal Year 2010 *(XLS, 82 KB)*
Supplemental Table 2	Persons Obtaining Legal Permanent Resident Status by Leading Core Based Statistical Areas (CBSAs) of Residence and Region and Country of Birth: Fiscal Year 2010 *(XLS, 76 KB)*
Supplemental Table 3	Persons Obtaining Legal Permanent Resident Status by Region of Birth and Core Based Statistical Area (CBSA) of Residence: Fiscal Year 2010 *(XLS, 72 KB)*
Supplemental Table 4	Immigrant-Orphans Adopted by U.S. Citizens by State or Territory of Residence, Gender, and Age: Fiscal Year 2010 *(XLS, 16 KB)*

This page was last reviewed / modified on March 30, 2011.